Hating To Love My Life

This book is a work of fiction. The names, characters and events in this book are the products of the author's imagination or are used fictitiously. Any similarity to real persons living or dead is coincidental and not intended by the author.

The views and opinions expressed in this book are solely those of the author and do not necessarily reflect the views or opinions of Gatekeeper Press. Gatekeeper Press is not to be held responsible for and expressly disclaims responsibility of the content herein.

Hating to Love My Life:
The Fighter in Me Would Not Let Me Die

Published by Gatekeeper Press
7853 Gunn Hwy, Suite 209
Tampa, FL 33626
www.GatekeeperPress.com

Copyright © 2022 by Courtlin D. Fields
All rights reserved. Neither this book, nor any parts within it may be sold or reproduced in any form or by any electronic or mechanical means, including information storage and retrieval systems, without permission in writing from the author. The only exception is by a reviewer, who may quote short excerpts in a review.

The editorial work for this book is entirely the product of the author. Gatekeeper Press did not participate in and is not responsible for any aspect of this element.

Library of Congress Control Number: 2022950612

ISBN (paperback): 9781662934902

Hating To Love My Life

*The Fighter in Me
Would Not Let Me Die*

Courtlin D. Fields

gatekeeper press™
Tampa, Florida

Thank you, GOD for never allowing me to give up on myself.

Dedication

Grandmother Josephine Fernandez – Forever my shining light.
I do miss our conversations while playing spades and your famous line.
"You cut my cat, I'll cut your dog".

Forever in my heart: *Dad, Cora, Patricia, Alexander, Kent, Leodis, Evelyn, Ricky, Stanley, Richard, Nanna, Mrs. Robinson*

My God-Mother Mary: My biggest lesson thus far.
I will never wait to see or to say I love you to anyone again. (RIP)

My mom set the foundation with one life lesson: She said Derrick I am not whipping your ass for stealing. I am whipping your ass because you got caught. Never take on or do anything if you are not a master at it. Because then you would not have got caught.
(If you're not from Brownsville or a rough neighborhood you may not understand)
From that day moving forward. I never stole again.

Sister 1 Always took my punishment;
Sister 2 Always made me fight for anything I wanted.
Sister 3 My sense of style & hustle.

Uncle Nate Thank you for being there.

To the people who believed, pushed, and always supported me.
This is not in know order.

Anthony, Carlton, Keith, Walter, Nate Jr, Kim, William, Eric Ramos and family, Bobby, Clearance, Dead eye, Ruby Red, Octavius (RIP) **Monica, Re-Re, Stacey, Tamika, Tammi, Victoria, Tisha, Darrell, DeP, Eric T, Famecia, Gilot, Hadley** (if it wasn't for you, I would not be able to walk again). **Jade, Jay** (RIP) **John, J'rome** (wow always keeping me encouraged). **Keenan and the Slade family. Kilvin** (RIP) **Quincy, Rowan, Teasha, Titus, Danna,** and **Verlon. Pretty Del, Cynthia, Roslyn, Regina, Randy, Ronald, Leslie, Saundra, Sue, Jay, Andrew, John, Adam Legrand, Roy, Jefferey, Liz, Shawn Bebe, Monique, Ronald jr, Erica, Eric, Jerome, Elizabeth, Darlene, Lakim, Tina**

To my Children, I really can't think of what to express because you are more than paper you are more than words. You are my life and I love you all.

To the COURTYAYA Inc Team, Fields-Caffe Team, Brooklyn, Brownsville, New York, Freeport, and to all Family & Friends I missed

Thank You

Contents

My Mission Statement 1

RESILIENCE part 1 3

RESILIENCE part 2 7

Self-encouragement (Revenge) 11

I AM 15

Not Meant To Be 17

Body of Prayer 19

CAN'T FIND LOVE 21

The Last Time 23

NOT Enough 25

Lost Playing Games 27

Confusing Confessions	31
Not My Home	35
Knowing You Had Gone	39
PAUSE	43
On Purpose	47
Thoughts Getting in the Way	51
BLACKNESS	53
LIGHTSKIN	55
SURVIVING	59
Fighting For My Life	61
Season Heart Bullshit	63

My Mission Statement

Today I Arise with no promises of being here tomorrow.
With uncertainties of what today may bring.
I arise today grateful & humbled.

Knowing GOD gave ME another chance to
continue today or walk away from my yesterday.

I arise freely by HIS will knowing my freedom of choice to
not let the burden of my yesterday weigh me down.
To conquer my freedom to live today.

I arise knowing the true testament
in my pain, my sorrow, and the ones I lost were defeated.
I stand before you to tell the story of how I arrived when
I Arise

RESILIENCE *part 1*

People often tell me you can't beat life.
Life will always win.
Life will keep on going.
There is no stopping life.

For the longest time, I had imagined life was like this amazing fighter.
One of the greats like
Ali, Ray, Mike, or Floyd.
But he wasn't, he wasn't like anything I imagine.
He was undefeated & never lost.
This time he was whipping my ass.

I could not land one single punch.
Every time I got up. This thing, this supernatural kept knocking me down until one day he almost landed a fatal punch.
I was out for the count.
I had no idea how I was going to live.
It seemed I had no one in my corner.

When you get hit so many times you start to lose hope and focus.
I can hear life telling me
"Stay down". It's over".

I just wanted to die.
I let everyone down.
My peers, my family including my kids.
Friends would say hi to me with shame.
I was a disgrace.

Continued onto the next page...

Now I am here alone once again.
This thing called life knows my every move.
Every time I get up, He's there.
I go left, he's there, I go right, he is there.
Every time he appears

He's hitting me harder. This last TKO I knew I was done.
I was going to die!
He hit me with some old combo shit.
Life hit me so hard that my father felt it & died.
Family, friends, and even at work all felt it.
That combo landed; I thought I threw up my hands.

I couldn't understand why I couldn't win.
I couldn't understand why he was fighting me so hard
With everything, he's got.
Why? why is he fighting me so hard?
What did I do to deserve this punishment?

Nothing I said or did was good enough.
I was losing so bad it felt like GOD gave up on me.
I believe I met GOD once in a dream & he kicked me out.
That's how low I became.
I felt like I had nothing else to lose.
GOD doesn't want me; the world is against me and
Life is trying to kill me
I give up!

RESILIENCE *part 2*

Suddenly something happened,
something transformed me.

I felt a jolt in my spirit.
Here I am at my lowest point
and a strong voice called out
      " Get up"!
It was the craziest feeling ever.

I mean Life had knocked me down
and I always got up.
But I never got up in such a way
that I was determined.
To figure out what is Life secret.

What is it he does not want me to see?
This isn't like chess or spades.
Where Life deals you a hand and you deal with it.
Nah I'm not going to give up just yet.
You piqued my interest.
"One more round, all of nothing".

      Ding, Ding, Ding

Focus, stay in the moment.
Don't waste your energy.
Don't try to win, just block, block guard yourself.
Wait for your opening. He is getting tired,
he is getting tired,
wait for it. Wait for, wait for it.... now... Blackout.

Continued onto the next page...

Opening of me pushing through the dark heavy doors.
The high sign says, "Dreams Come True".
Push open another set of dark doors.
High sign of Fields-Caffe.

Walking through pushing open another set of doors
To see COURTYAYA INC PRODUCTION...

Push through and open a lighter set of doors.
Enter family and friends...
It All starts with You!!!!

Resilience

Self-encouragement (Revenge)

Although you are hurting at this moment.
Take the time to understand this moment.
Think of what went wrong and let it go.
Think of what went right and hold on.
Embrace this moment by feeling all the emotions.
We will react and that's truly a fact.

You have been down before
The players have changed
But the game still remains the same.

What you going through is not a loss.
After all, this is your fault.
Yes! they caught you slippin:
But you're not trippin.
You allowed them to slide when
You know the card they played was not allowed.

But that's your heart.
It's never a loss when you give a
person a place to start.
You took a chance and I am proud of you.

Now get on up because this loss was a setup
For your great come-up.
We don't weaken
We don't crumble
We may fall
But we for dam sure don't crawl.

Continued onto the next page...

Every action has a reaction
Yeah we've been down before
The players have changed
But the game remains the same
Now show these mofos who you are
Once and for all.
Now GO get the bag
BECAUSE THE MOMENT OF SUCCESS
AT ITS BEST
WHEN IT'S SERVED AS YOUR REVENGE

I AM

In my life I am great
In my life I am destined
In my life, I am someone you should know
In my life, I am someone you should never hate.

I am the author of my life
I am the creator of my day to day
I am not the promise of tomorrow
But I am the challenge that may come my way.

If you want to get to know me
Then really get to know me.
For only then you will get to see
I am whom I say I am.

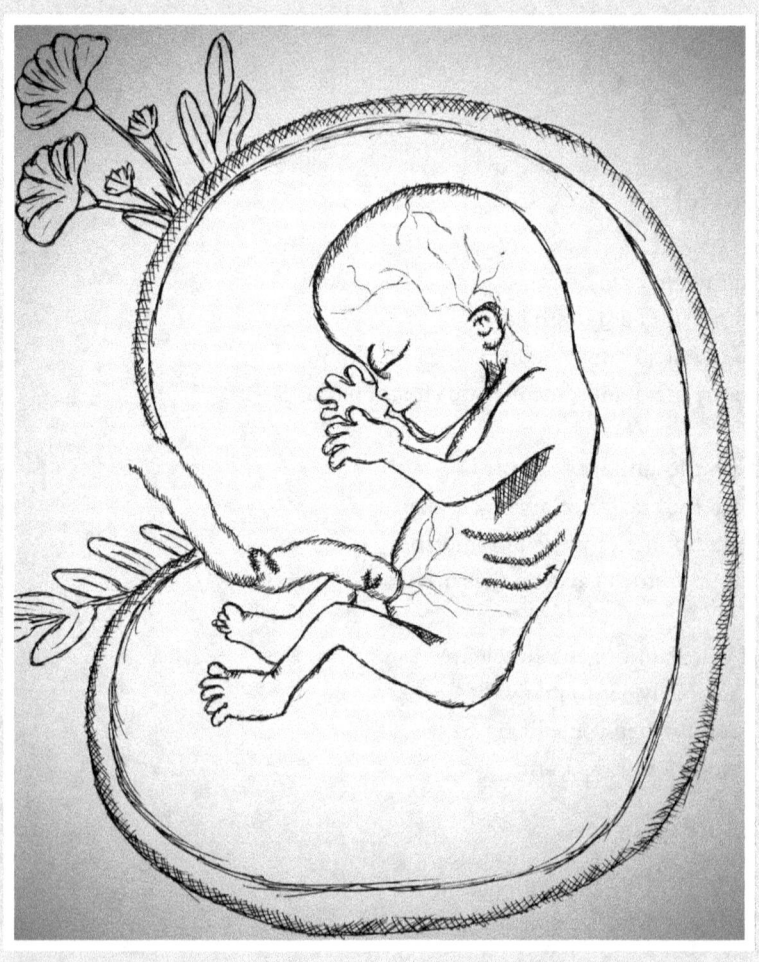

Not Meant To Be

The escape of the day is what is anticipated.
The hurt that one of the few causes for the betterment of their behalf.
The ocean breeze heals the lonely cries as if they know my pain.
It is with my heart I cry
It is with my love I cry
It is with my soul that dies
That ocean breeze fades me
For you will always be with me
A dad to you was not meant to be.

Body of Prayer

GOD give me the hands that can touch so many lives
Give me the heart to love, be loved & most of all accept love with
every relationship that starts

Give me the feet to balance my life when it seems out of control
GOD give me the legs to stand on to walk these open roads
Give the arms to help pull me up day to day
for this mountain is no race just something to get over to fill your
grace

Give me the voice to speak with compassion.
From my lips be taught not to speak
but to listen with my ears for no judgment comes without fears.

Bless my mind to be wise
and only get better in time
like fine wine.

Teach my eyes to see
and not give in to idealism and false hope.
For my eyes were blind but with you
dear LORD, I am able to see.

GOD heal my back
for the stab wounds are deep
for it was those whom I didn't see
that tried to knock me off my feet.

But most of all GOD
strengthens my heart
for my soul is the root that leads to the center of YOUR core.

CAN'T FIND LOVE

Can't find love in no real-time bliss
Can't find love in no small-town bliss
Can't find love by turning around.
SURE, can't find love by slowing down.

I tried to call but my love wouldn't answer
I tried to find it, but it was not lost
because I never had it.
I thought I had love maybe twice in my life.
But that ended in divorce so it couldn't have mattered.

I ask GOD to send me love
To hold and cherish.
Let them not cheat or take advantage.

Love wants to give me what "LOVE" want me to have
Too fat, too thin, nope that's not a win.
Personality, the charm, the laugh I mean
The one that makes you pass gas.

But GOD hasn't sent anything,
just meeting people with a whole bunch of baggage
to add to the others, I thought that mattered.

Can't find love in no real-time bliss
Can't find love in no small-town bliss
Can't find love by running around.
Sure, can't find love-

oh, wait who is this?
Oh, it's you.
Come in Love & tell me why you matter.

The Last Time

If I am what you want
Forgive me as if it's the last time

Look at me as if it's the last time
Touch me as if it's the last time
Say my name as if it's the last time

Tell me I am yours as if it's the last time
Tell me you'll miss me as if it's the last time
Hold me as if it is the last time.

Make Love to me as if it's the last time
Let's fuck as if it's the last time
Let me taste you as if it's the last time
Dance with me as if it's the last time
Let's laugh together as if it's the last time

Let's say I love you as if it's the last time
Let's cry together as if it's the last time
Because when it's all said and done
this could be our very last time.

NOT Enough

It's not enough
It's not enough to be important to myself
It's not enough to wake up every morning to the same face steering
back at me in the mirror.

I want to be important to you
I want to exist in a fearless love
With no compromises or broken promises.

In consideration of the inconsistency
of being varied as unimportant of this
a disillusioned love affair.

Lost Playing Games

I let love go one too many times before.
Playing games of whose calling who first.
I can't be the one to show my feelings first.

Just dying inside of thirst.
We often say how come
you didn't say or
you never told me
because of our lack of mistrust
within ourselves.

Trying to play this perfect guy
hiding the real me buried inside.
Dam Why am I so shy?

Not knowing if I am myself
you can see the real me & say yes
by giving me. Yes Me!
A try to be your guy.

To pretend is a lie; to lie is to pretend.
Giving off false illustrations is
to lie and lie again.

Thinking back on how I was so wrong
by not being upfront and standing strong
Now I sit here weathering the many storms.

Continued onto the next page...

Now I am labeled a mistrust,
only out because of my lust.
Playing the same game
time & time again
keeping the real me hostage within.

While the fake-ass me is
left in the dust blaming everybody
else but myself.

Not this time around, no game-playing for me.
I'm going to keep it real & show you who I will really be.

Confusing Confessions

I hate that I like you so much
I hate that I wake up; I think about you
I hate when I go to sleep, I think about you
I hate that part of my day
I am thinking of the future of me & you
I hate it, I hate it, I hate it!

You will tell me hi once in a blue. I hate it!
You know what to say and when to say it. I hate it!
The words you speak keep me going for weeks. I hate it!
I cannot express myself because I don't want you to know you got me wrapped
And then you leave me. I hate it!

Your big mistakes, I can look away.
But the ones that love me; cannot get away with shit.
I hate it! I hate it! I hate it!

You are my poison,
you're an Addiction
I need to get rid of
I hate I need to get rid of you.
I hate it, I hate it, I hate it

How come the things that make you feel so good,
Is the very essence which is the wrong thing for you.
Those are the very things that will destroy you.
I hate it.

Continued onto the next page...

I hate not knowing what true love feels like.
I hate not being able to give true love.
I hate it, I hate it

I hate you for making me feel
like you are giving me true love.
What I hate most; is not knowing what true love feels.

So how do I know if you really love me?
I don't and I hate it.

Not My Home

This is not my home anymore
All that is left is the empty
walls of when we first met.
I told you; you'll be mine &
I'll be yours. Nothing but
GOD will come between us.

Hard to believe this is not my home anymore.

I touched you there and touch you there
blessing the walls from corner to corner
without harm or danger.

I can't believe this is not home anymore.

You caressed my mind, giving my body,
heart & my comfort throughout the night.
From the tender tears, we often cried out,
to the fussing & fights that only you would know about.
Up & down these twisted stairs
just like my life. One way up & one way down.
Different exits lead us all to the ground floor.

I can't believe this is not home anymore.

Lonely nights filled my eyes,
looking at street cars passing by.
A Dip in your wetness made the day less shade,
giving that relief of tension & not to mention
the body looks right because of the creation
of what was missing in the explanation.

Continued onto the next page...

I can't believe this is not home anymore.

For your walls have gone cold,
the touch is strange as if I'm passed by.
I feel a draft coming over me.
Just like my lonely heart.

I can't believe this right here is not my home anymore.
Goodnight

Knowing You Had Gone

I went to bed knowing you had gone.
Replaying the incident
over and over again in my head.
Counting the times of your many goodbyes.
But realizing this goodbye you were gone.

I woke up this morning knowing you had gone.
Memories filled the air of the mistreatment
and misrepresentation of who you are
became very clear.

In deciding your mental dysfunctional truth
was not at all times there.
Yeah, I woke up this morning knowing you were gone.

Feelings of me being ashamed of my triumphant
of making and encouraging you to be great was my doubt.
But the difference between yesterday versus today.
I woke up knowing you were gone.

Cleaned the house of every lie,
every foul thing that came out your mouth.
The childish games of pettiness are wack.
Trying to help you while my life is going off track.

Painted the walls with a fresh coat.
Remodel the area of what used to be you right there.

Praising GOD for no regrets on how it got there.
But humbled enough to say GOD I do declare.

Continued onto the next page...

Huh... yeah... I woke up this morning knowing you were gone.
Everyone concerned, can't quite understand,
clutching their pearls in their hand.
Ask themselves how could it be
less then 24 hours I have mourned
and I all ready to move on.

IT WAS SIMPLE & VERY EASY

I loved you with all my might.
Did everything I could to make things right,
sometimes that meant me going without.
I have no regrets about the love I put out.
I gave you my love free of charge.
Even though towards the end
it became really, really, really dam hard.
I woke up this morning knowing you were gone.

You gave up on Free pure love from me,
So, everything I had done with everything I did,
came straight from my heart.

You said I was vengeful
and how right you are.
Revenge is in the eyes of the beholder.
Go on and get out.
Let's see who is going to give your love a free handout.

Yes! it is easy for me to mourn and move on.
Because I woke up this morning knowing you were gone.

PAUSE

I had to take pause on me to look at you.
To realize it had nothing to do with me
and my reality.
But it was much to do with you.

Your fixation on the blame game
manipulating the words
To fulfill your personal and deviant gains.

Your anger arose not of me personally
but it arose
of the person I became
and you sort so desperately to be.

I had to take pause on me to look at you.
In the beginning, we were so much alike.
Our views, treasured moments
to the deepest secrets,
we kept from the world,
stood more than just a sentiment.

It had value.
That was the connection
The disconnect came from you,
not able to understand
How I could connect to deal with my problems.

The lonely hurt for so many years
through the pain
and the constant tears of my sorrow.

Continued onto the next page...

Your anger rose with thorns
to prick anything to dare to come close.
Protecting yourself
from the shame & humiliation of it all.

I had to take pause on me to look at you.
You don't hate me: you don't despise me.
The Envy you convey is not of the person you see.
It's the person you stop fighting to be.

On Purpose

It feels like I have the flu.
Every part of me hurts.
Tender to the touch.
But it's not you. IT- IS - ME.

I sort after you, on purpose!
I told people that I wanted you, on purpose!
I met with you, on purpose!
I dated you, on purpose!
And even when you told me you were leaving

I kissed you, on purpose!
I wanted to get to know you, on purpose!
I allowed myself to share with you, on purpose!
I opened up to you, on purpose!
I argued with you, on purpose!
I played with you, on purpose!
And even when you told me you were leaving.

I cared for you, on purpose!
I laid down with you, on purpose!
I fell for you, on purpose!
IM-IN-LOVE-YOU on purpose!!!
Because you have been so honest with me from the
beginning, that you are leaving

Continued onto the next page...

I suffer for you, on purpose!
I am HAPPY for you, on purpose!
I am PROUD of you, on purpose!
But it does not stop my heart from hurting for you,
On purpose!
I did this to myself, on purpose!
If you ask me if I regret it or would, do it all over again.
I would say YES 100x all over again and it will be done
On purpose!

Every moment I spent with you was on purpose.
I rather have been with you than not experiencing life
without you, because then my life would of
FELT - LIKE - IT - HAD - NO PURPOSE!!!

Thoughts Getting in the Way

I thought I was strong until someone I loved walked out my life.
I thought I was weak until I picked myself up after a falling dream.
I thought I was brave until I walked out on my own.
I thought I was fearless until not having you made me scared.
I thought I knew everything until you stop talking to me.
I thought I can face anything until you stood in front of me.
I thought I needed no one until you showed me I needed you.
I thought I was nothing until you spoke to me and said:

You were my everything the day I created you.

Now I know my thoughts were nothing until I humbled myself to you LORD

AMEN AMEN AMEN.

BLACKNESS

I am a black man trying to survive and be free.
I live in the ghetto part of white society.
I fear for my life, and I fear for yours too
But tell me black brother what can I do?

I am just one brother trying to change all
But it's brothers like you who keep building the wall.

Can you read can you write?
No, you say, you steal, sell drugs and you fight.
Right on black brother, right on!

It's okay if you take my brothers and sisters away
It's okay if they're lying in the street day after day.
And
Truly okay to blame the white man.

But look close real closely. It's the color of your hand
Who is killing our children, mothers, and our fathers?
We escaped slavery and believe me. We'll escape crack cocaine too.
Because
We are a Black nation who came too far and fought too long

LIGHTSKIN

Why do you keep beating me
for the color of my skin?
Is it not fair enough to blend in?

Why do you mark me with shame
and call me out my name?
Do you think that I too don't feel pain?

Was it I who rape Mrs.?
Or settled down for all the fine richest?
Or am I the one who always gets blamed
for whatever the cost for my
mother to bear me a name?

A name for which you have not called me
but labeled me because of my past
generational hurt and pain the ole age Master proclaim
And now I must bear the shame.

Piss boy, Colored boy, yellow boy
and if I am lucky,
I just may hear boy.

I used to blame GOD for giving me the color of the sun.
But my faith has taught me
that I am still his son.

You kick & spit at me.
Beat me to the point I will rise no more.
Just remember the same GOD that created you and much more
did not make me the color you so righteously adore.

Continued onto the next page...

I see both sides of the color
of whose is right and who is to blame.
Before you raise your hand &
before you pass judgment
just remember
I am your son, your brother your father, and your teacher.
I am a friend from an enemy born into sin.
I am a lover of people whom
GOD created the world we all live in.

SURVIVING

TODAY IAM ALONE ONCE AGAIN
MY MOTHER, SISTER, OR MY FRIENDS CAN NOT HELP ME
NO! NOT A ONE, NOBODY CAN HELP ME WIN
WITH THIS FEAR THAT IS IN MY HEART

I TO DO STRUGGLE, TO DO THE SAME
THAT YOU HAVE DONE TO ME
TO TAKE AWAY YOUR PRIDE AND
YOUR SENSE OF BEING FREE

NO! NOT A ONE, NOBODY CAN HELP ME WIN
WITH THIS FEAR THAT IS IN MY HEART

I HAVE LEARNED LIFE RIGHTS AND WRONGS
I HAVE LEARNED GOD'S WAY TOO
BUT IN THIS SOCIETY OF CRACK, COCAINE, ROBBERS
MURDERERS, RAPIST, AND MOST OF ALL RACISM
WHAT IS A PERSON SUPPOSED TO DO

NO! NOT A ONE CAN HELP ME WIN
WITH THIS FEAR I HAVE IN MY HEART

OH, PLEASE DEAR LORD, PLEASE HELP ME
NOT TO FALL APART
I AM CRYING FROM THE DEPTHS OF MY SOUL
WITH THE BLOOD RUSHING RAPIDLY IN MY HEART
HOLDING ON TO WHATEVER PRIDE I HAVE LEFT IN
MY FREEDOM SONG

AND I WILL TELL YOU THIS, THAT (I) WILL LAST
YES, I WILL LAST LONG. I WILL BE THE LAST BIRD
STANDING TALL AND STRONG

Fighting For My Life

I'm fighting for my life
I'm fighting for my life when people don't believe me.
I'm fighting for my health while praying to GOD, he grants me one more breath.
Fighting the mentals that are raiding my temple.
Breaking the walls of my Spirit.

Fighting the tears to save face to present myself that I am okay.
The forcefield is down.
My heart & soul is on the ground.
The battle for Blessings seems too far to reach.
Every day the war continues but my freedom song is living long.

Fighting is getting too hard to bear on my own.
I'm searching for my FATHER to help me move on.
Fighting to listen to his voice.
But the battle in my head drowns out even his song.
So, I pray he hears my voice for I know he is my source of power to help me to my feet.
Hear my voice FATHER give me the strength to weather the storm.
For my fight is lost if I am not to hear your voice.

Season Heart Bullshit

I loved you with my whole heart
The purity of my love I gave without
Hesitation not for a single doubt.

Stricken with the sickness of your insecurities
You left me broken
The world I once knew is fallen apart.

You broke me
left here picking up the pieces.
Without a clear sign or clue.
Just "I am too much for you".
At what point were you going to tell your truth?

I was upfront right from the very start.
Never questioning your role,
I never knew you were playing a part.

Man, women, women, man
Same-sex who gives a dam
You are all wrong when I hear
people come into your
life for a season bullshit
Not when it comes to a person's heart.

I could understand if we grew apart
But your phony ass can't tell the truth.
You want me to forgive you.
When I am in the dark?

This is no teenage crush or
20's when your experiencing matters of the heart.
We are in our 30s and you are relying on
the universe to figure it all out.

Continued onto the next page...

Fuck your season
Fuck your journey
I am not the weather.
I am human!
A human with a heart.
Now broken, because your dysfunctional
Ass could not be truthful from the start.

You have been listening to illogical for far too long.
Not grasping the season's concept
since people seem to forget.
The seasons are consistent
They come around once every year.

They have highs and they have lows.
Just depends on when the sunrise
And which way the wind blows
There are storms, hurricanes, and tsunami
Whatever it is going through
It will remain the season.

It is consistent. The fact I am persistent
I already know how to prepare.
I can always count on the seasons
to be there every dam year.
You or no one else gets
a pass on my heart.
Now that's foul on your Bullshit.

www.ingramcontent.com/pod-product-compliance
Lightning Source LLC
LaVergne TN
LVHW011857060526
838200LV00054B/4376